What People Are Saying About *Subprime Real Estate Profits...*

"Thank you for providing such wonderful tools for learning how to do effective marketing. Thank you for giving me the "shot in the arm" that I needed to get myself in gear! You are truly one of God's angels here on earth!"

- Darlene Domar, Buffalo Grove, IL –

"Rachel's attention to detail and ability to hit the nail on the head every time is unbelievable! Anyone who takes advantage of your material is DEFENITELY in for more than they expect! I tell everyone I can about you!"

- Glenn Shepard, Nashville, TN #1 Barnes & Noble Best Seller -

"Thanks very much for the investing tips. By the way, I really found your book very informative for subprime marketing. I learned some new tricks that I wasn't aware of or just reminded of. "

- Jackie Davis, St. Louis, MO -

"By jove I think you've got it!! Many thanks for hitting the mark so perfectly."

-Bruce and Trisha Crespo, Huntington, NY-

"As we all know the first step in buying real estate is making offers to sellers. When more sellers are calling, more offers are being written. The real estate market in this country is saturated with investors out there sending letters. Ask yourself this, "Why will they open mine and respond". The answer, use the techniques that successful investors like Rachel in a very competitive market have had success with."

-Dylan Tanaka, Detroit Suburbs, MI-

"Thankfully I have been able to take just ONE piece of Rachel's advice and DOUBLED my motivated seller response rate! I can't wait to see what else she has in store!"

-Steve Kansa, Duluth, GA-

"I would like to thank you for all the help and support that you have provided me in marketing my Real Estate business. You have a very good grasp on what makes the sellers pick up the phone and make the first call. You bring to your organization a wealth of experience from your own Real Estate business and it shows very clearly in your professional approach to problem solving.

- Nikhil Sawant, Cumming, GA-

Subprime Real Estate Profits

How to Become a Millionaire in 18 Months or Less Using Subprime Real Estate!

Rachel Young

Visit our website at www.subprimesecrets.com

Printed in the United States of America

ISBN 0-9796396-0-3

Book designed by Paul Perdue of Perdue Vision

FREE! – A Special Bonus Gift!

As our way of saying thank you for taking an active role in your success education, we have made an additional bonus gift available to you. Worth $47.97, this special gift is yours to keep FREE as a reader of Subprime Real Estate Profits.

All you have to do to get your bonus gift is visit our special website at: www.bigcheesemarketing.com/27-things.htm and the gift is yours FREE. Thank you and enjoy reading!

This book is dedicated to all the individuals who were told they 'can't' but did it all anyway. You can do so much more than you know and I believe in you!

ACKNOWLEDGEMENTS:

To my mother and father, Fred and Nancy – For setting a consummate example of what two loving parents should be. For instilling in me those traits and attributes I have utilized to get where I am today; honesty, integrity, respect, and discipline. Thank you most of all for teaching me to believe in myself and showing me that the sky truly is the limit.

To Glenn and Cindy Shepard – Your support and encouragement have spurred me on to be and do more than I even thought possible!

To Jason Oman – Your guidance, instruction, and assistance in creating this book is immeasurable. Anyone that doesn't use your techniques to create their own #1 Best-Seller is settling for second best!

To my children – I couldn't possibly ask for better. You guys put up with a lot of crazy days and even crazier moods. Please know that everything I do, I do it because of you guys. I love you more than life itself.

Most of all, to my husband John – You are my partner, my best friend, my soul mate. I cannot imagine life without you. You've indulged all of my harebrained ideas and suggestions, allowed me to chase every dream, and still managed to keep me grounded. This would not be possible without you. I love you more each day. Thank you just doesn't seem like enough.

Contents

Foreword

Introduction

Chapter 1 - Good Girls Don't Get Fired!....................................17

Always Have a Backup Plan!,18

Subprime Real Estate Lesson #1,21

Something to Think About,22

Chapter 2 – Good Girls Can't Be Homeless!....................................23

You Can Go Farther Than You Think!,27

How Does This Apply To Subprime Real Estate?,29

Chapter 3 – Good Girls Don't Get Sued!..37

Why Don't They Teach Life in College?,42

The Intimidation Factor,46

Chapter 4 – A Basement Full of Crap..51

When Life Gives You Manure,52

My Dad Always Said,55

Chapter 5 – The Subprime Opportunity's Knocking!....................................59

What is Subprime?, 60

Subprime Statistics,62

Chapter 6 – Decisions, Decisions,

Decisions!..69

Who's Afraid of the BBB?,73

Chapter 7 – Getting the Phone to Ring..79

One Letter, One Situation,84

Chapter 8 – Graduate Magna Cum Laude of the School of Hard Knocks!....................87

Chapter 9 – Subprime Secrets..................89

Whatdya get?,93

How Much Would You Pay?,97

What Motivates You More?, 101

Recommended Resources.....................105

A Special Free Gift from the Author........107

Foreword

Dear Reader,

On a beautiful late spring afternoon, ten years ago, two young women graduated from the same high school.

They were very much alike, these two young women.

Both had been better than average students, both were personable, and - as young high school graduates are - both were filled with ambitious dreams for the future.

Recently, these women returned to their high school for their ten year reunion...

They were still very much alike.

Both were married with three children. And both, it turned out, had begun dabbling in Real Estate at some point in their careers and were still actively involved.

But there was a difference.

One of the women was still struggling to pay her bills each month. The other was a millionaire.

Have you ever wondered, as I have, what makes this kind of difference in people's lives?

The difference cannot be found in native intelligence or talent or dedication. It's not that one person wants success and the other person doesn't.

The difference lies in what each person knows and how he or she makes use of that knowledge.

Now, in the pages of this book you're reading, you'll discover the kind of knowledge that makes all the difference in the world.

Your future will be very exciting indeed. As you begin to learn and apply the brilliant information Rachel Young shares with you throughout this book.

Go forth and prosper, my friend!

We'll see you at the top!

Jason Oman
#1 International Best-Selling Author of Conversations with Millionaires

Introduction

THERE'S A DIFFERENCE BETWEEN NEW INVESTORS AND SEASONED INVESTORS. I think everybody knows that, but when it comes to marketing there is an even bigger difference between new and seasoned investors!

New investors hear the gurus talk on stage about how easy it is to get involved in real estate, they'll teach you the latest and greatest way to buy and sell houses, and they'll tell you that the leads are all going to be in your mailbox tomorrow morning...and it doesn't happen that way. They'll tell you that the leads are going to magically appear and they don't.

But as seasoned investors, a lot of times, we have a tendency to get complacent in the number of leads that we're getting. We're chugging right along and don't really see a need to up our game any.

There's nobody there to push us to make us uncomfortable and keep yelling, "You can do even more! Don't stop now!" And sometimes, as seasoned investors, myself included, we have a tendency to think that I know it all, and we don't. I'm probably the only woman that's going to admit that to you. (If my husband was reading this, he'd be clapping too.)

If you looked at the top 100 most powerful and influential people of the 20th century...we're talking Florence Nightingale, Winston Churchill, Martin Luther King Jr., and Mahatma Gandhi, 75% of them either grew up in an impoverished family, were abused as children or had some form of mental or physical deficiency.

Why do you think that is? **Because they weren't willing to settle.** They knew that there was something better out there and they kept pushing and kept pushing! That's one of the many topics we're going to talk about during our time together.

Chapter 1

Good Girls Don't Get Fired!

SEVERAL YEARS AGO, I WAS WORKING FOR THE LARGE PHONE COMPANY THAT USED TO BE LOCATED IN ATLANTA. That's where I'm from. My division was responsible for getting this particular phone company long distance and we had a huge party. Oh my goodness we celebrated.

Two weeks later we had another huge party. The party where they said "Thanks so much, have a nice day!"

But the union was supposed to protect us! The union was going to help us keep our jobs!

All of a sudden I found myself with no job. Not only did I not have a job...I was also going through, I think it's fair to say, a pretty nasty divorce at the time. I came home from my last day at work to find the house completely gutted and my children were gone.

For the next 6 months I searched for my children. I have 3 children, right now the oldest is going to be 11 in 3 days and the twins are 6. At the time, they were teeny tiny. I didn't know if they were alive or dead, if they even knew I wasn't there! I didn't know anything. I couldn't find them anywhere. It turns out they were in North Carolina, but we'll get to that in a minute.

I tell this story because the first thing I learned dealt a lot with my own personal life-education.

Always have a backup plan!

Never go into something thinking that plan A is the way that everything is going to turn out, because that's not the way it works. Plan A often winds up being Plan C, or Plan X, or Plan M.

You're going to see – this is just the tip of the iceberg! The thing that kept me going was 'massive action'...sort of. I would insert one more word in there that will completely change the dynamic of it and is in fact the system that we use to get out of every single situation that I'm going to talk about today.

Its three words. Massive, simultaneous action. (It should be noted that I didn't call it this at the time. We just knew we needed to do everything within our power to get the heck out of a bad place! It wasn't until several years later that a mentor of mine, Dan Kennedy, put what we did into those three words.)

We're a society that likes to plan for the most part. Right? You go from step one to step two to step three and eventually you get to the end result, where you make money.

The problem is, if you keep doing that we're all going to be in a bunch of retirement homes at the end of the day, having only got one major thing accomplished. Massive, simultaneous action, that's the key.

Without massive, simultaneous action, I'd still be getting ready to get ready. Right? As a matter of fact, it's not even ready, aim, fire; it's not even ready, fire, aim. Its fire and then everything else is secondary. Fire first, clean up the mess later. It's much easier to ask forgiveness than it is permission. So always have a backup plan.

How do you apply that to subprime real estate?

You've got to have more than one house-buying strategy in your arsenal. Let me ask you this, if you knew that there was a mouse in your house, would you set out just one trap to catch it? Or would you bait the kitchen so that it looked like a Tom and Jerry episode where everywhere you step, you're tripping over a mouse trap.

You're not going to use just one strategy to buy and sell houses. There are people out there that can teach you all the latest and greatest ways to buy and sell real estate, but you've got to have more than one buying strategy. The key is knowing your 'risk tolerance' and choosing what strategy works best for YOU.

I'll give you an example. I was going to meet with Sally Seller one time and my primary buying strategy at the time was 'subject to'...where I take over the seller's debt, buy the property in a land trust and make the payments to the lender for the seller until I sell the house.

Over the phone, Sally says she's fine with that. She said "Yeah that sounds great." And when I get out to meet her, she says "I don't know that I'm willing to let you make my payments for me with the loan staying in my name".

I had to dig into my investment bag and pull out the 'sandwich lease option' strategy because I knew that was going to appease her and help me be able to get the deal to get going. Had I not had that in my arsenal, that would have been just yet another lead that I wasn't able to work on, so you always want to have more than one buying strategy.

Something to think about:

1. What are you doing to continuously educate yourself about real estate investing?

2. Have you taken the steps necessary in order to maximize the buying strategies in your arsenal?
3. Do you know those strategies well enough that if a seller wasn't sure about one option you presented them, that you'd be able to move to option 2 seamlessly?
4. What back up plans have you made for your investing company in order to prevent such 'bad situations' from occurring (and if they do occur, that they're only momentary)?
5. What 'massive simultaneous action' are you taking each day to generate seller leads for your business? Buyer leads? Private lender leads?
6. Is there something more you could be doing each day in order to generate the leads you WANT instead of 'just enough to get by'?

Chapter 3

Good Girls Can't Be Homeless!

OH MY GOODNESS, GOOD GIRLS CANT BE HOMELESS! That's a lie.

After I lost my job and I came home to find my children gone, I didn't care about anything. I didn't care about the way I looked, I didn't care if the bills were getting paid, I didn't care about cleaning the house, I didn't care about leaving the house. I definitely didn't care about eating. I didn't care about anything or anybody.

Why should I?

My 3 main motivating factors for getting out of bed in the morning were gone, and I didn't know where they were. Needless to say, the house went into foreclosure. As I'm literally sitting in my living room waiting for the sheriff to come and kick me out, I'm flipping through a book that I have no idea how it wound up in my house in the first place. It was Rich Dad/Poor Dad, by Robert Kiyosaki. The book that was responsible for getting most investors into real estate in the first place.

I'm reading Kiyosaki's book and watching the mail come in, and I'm starting to notice a trend in the way that the lender's letters are coming into my house.

I noticed each letter is getting more and more severe. Each letter is hitting more and more emotional buttons within me to guilt me into paying the lender and I got to thinking, "You know these guys are trying to get the very funds from me that are allowing my family, me, to live right now. If they can use this tactic to get money from someone like me, what could I do to help people in my same situation?" I thought about it, butd I didn't know what I was going to do. Literally I was waiting for the knock on the door for the Sheriff to come and just start chucking my stuff out into the yard.

Ultimately, I wound up living in my car for a while. I was on my way to the hospital, 6 months later to have them either commit me or put me on some kind of medication because I couldn't take it any more.

You see, mothers of 3 do not wind up living in their car, with no job, no way to pay any kind of bills, credit like you would not believe, I think I may be the first person in history to have a credit score of 2, okay? It was bad. Good girls don't do that. And yet here I was. It all went against everything that I ever learned before.

You Can Go Farther Than You Think!

My personal education was, that you can go farther and do more than you think! I was able to use my skills as a marketer, which I didn't even know that I had, to get money from folks to allow me to go to a couple of boot camps and buy a couple of home study courses and get myself out of that basement.

While still employed at the phone company, I met a man named John. A former Marine and all-around great guy, John and I became good friends. After the divorce was finalized, we started dating. Unfortunately, he moved to South Carolina to take a job with another telecommunications company after the lay-off from the phone company in Atlanta. We continued to enjoy a long-distance relationship for several months.

When John heard about the situation with the children, and where I was living...he moved back to Georgia to be with me. It turns out that he was the one that originally put the Rich Dad/Poor Dad book in my hands, and we decided to take on the world of real estate together.

Back in the basement, I would wake up sore from crying so hard the night before. I didn't know what I was going to do or how to get the kids back. Having John by my side meant THE WORLD to me and helped me cope with some really bad times.

While we were living there, my ex-husband called to say, "Hey, the kids are cramping my style, you can have them back". He delivered them with the clothes on their back, and that was it.

The government is paying for my food, I'm living in a 200 square foot basement, I don't know how I'm going to make ends meet, I'm feeling a tremendous amount of mommy guilt for not being able to provide for my family. (Not to mention the depression, anxiety, and constant worry...but we'll get to that in a minute.)

Utilizing the skills and resources I had at my disposal (aka the public library), we were able to get out within 18 months and move. Not into a regular house, but into the house of our dreams. It was because we could go farther and do more than we thought!

So how do you apply it to subprime real estate?

Quite simply, your mindset determines your bank account size. If you don't think that you deserve the money, it isn't going to come to you.

It's going to go to somebody who respects it, somebody who appreciates it, somebody who loves the way it feels in their hand. Somebody that knows that they deserve each and every penny that comes to them.

> Prepare your mind for the riches that are coming your way!
>
> Join the Big Cheese Inner Circle Gold Program to hear Rachel share monthly the latest and greatest marketing tools dedicated to increasing your bottom line!
>
> Sign up at www.bigcheesemarketing.com/inner-circle.htm

It's said that you attract what you think about most. Man, I had money on the brain every single second of every single day. So I'm going to give you guys some homework. I home school my kids, and I've gotten kind of good at giving homework too.

(Note again that this idea originally came from my mentor, Dan Kennedy. I just modified it a little.)

You know that junk drawer in your kitchen where like everything winds up? There's tape measures and Scotch tape and pens that don't work and pencils with no lead in them, and receipts and remote controls and screws and light bulbs and everything else.

Your homework is to go home and clean it out. I don't mean like organize it and make it all nice and neat. Clean it out. There should be nothing in that drawer.

And then you're going to go to the bank and you're going to pull out 100 bucks. (If I had asked you to do this 6 years ago, it would have been me telling you to pull out 600 bucks, I'm going to pull out about $5, because that's all I had.)

I want you to pull out $100...but not a $100 bill. I want it in 5's, in 10's, in singles. I want it to look like a lot, and I want you to stuff this drawer full of that 100 dollars. This is your cash drawer.

Every single night when you come home from work or from meeting with buyers and sellers, you chuck more money in that drawer, and you watch what happens. Now you all are going to think I'm nuts, but bear with me.

Money likes to be with other money. Money is attracted to other money. Something weird is going to happen. It's miraculous and I promise you this is going to work if you do. With the money that's in that drawer, and you see it every day, and you can put your hands on it and you can touch it, that money is going to start multiplying.

I wrote about this on my website (www.bigcheesemarketing.com) and I had this one guy write in and say "I can't believe people still believe this crap". Within 24 hours after that post went on my website someone wrote in and said "Hang on a second brother, my wife and I started doing this and we didn't have the tens and twenties that Rachel talked about, we did it with ones and fives, and were able to save up $115 in 30 days. We didn't have 2 nickels to rub together and now I can take my wife out for Valentine's Day for a nice dinner".

It happens, if you're willing to do it. So your homework is to have a money drawer and from now on, you're going to start attracting money to you.

So, I said that your mind set determines your bank account size and that you can go farther than you thought.

How much father do you think you could go if you had somebody screaming in your ear down the field, don't stop? Give me your very best! Don't quit! Don't give up! Give me your best! People in my Inner Circle group get that every month from me.

You are getting to see that even though I was homeless, I was jobless, the government was paying for my food and even then that wasn't enough.

There were several nights that I had to choose between having dinner and running my real estate business.

There were several nights that I had to go around hungry as a result. Your mind set is going to determine everything.

So I think things can't get any worse because of the situation that we're in. When my children came home, they were all 15 pounds overweight for the 6 months that they had been gone. That, that's what happens when you eat pop tarts for breakfast, lunch and dinner. There were dental issues like you wouldn't believe!

My kids were violently afraid of the dark. They had separation anxiety issues. When I would take my oldest son to school he would say to me "You are coming back to get me, aren't you"? We pulled them out of public school and decided to home school.

John and I had also decided to get married. It makes all the difference in the world when you find the person you're SUPPOSE to be with! We knew from Day 1 that we were meant to be together forever.

We got married at the local courthouse just a week after my birthday.

Back in the basement, I'm thinking things are going finally going to be ok, I'm mean they could be worse. We could still be living in a car. But the fact of the matter was we were still in the basement. We'd bought and sold a couple of houses, we're just getting our feet wet and then the next thing happened.

This was the one I never saw coming and had one of the most profound affects on my husband and I during our time in that basement.

Chapter 3

Good Girls Don't Get Sued!

ONE NIGHT, I HEAR A KNOCK ON THE FRONT DOOR. It was a process server. And he handed me some paperwork. He said "Ms. Young, you're being sued."

I'd bought a house the wrong way, bought it subject to. We signed the deed at the kitchen table rather than closing in an attorney's office. I was doing what I'd been taught, but had failed to do my own 'due diligence'. The sellers were behind on payments and the house was facing foreclosure. I had negotiated with the bank to get the foreclosure stopped. I can't tell you what bank it was because we are still in litigation, and as of the writing of this book, it happened over 5 years ago.

The fact of the matter was, that the lender had assured me that they had stopped the foreclosure. Keep in mind, we were still very, very young in our investment career. For me the bank saying, "No really, we stopped the foreclosure!" was good enough for me.

So we borrowed $30,000 of my husband's parent's money to fix up the house. They owned a farm in South Carolina and sold a couple of cattle to get us the money to be able to rehab this house. We took that $30,000 and we rehabbed the property, based on the bank saying, "No really, we stopped the foreclosure, everything's fine."

In the mean time I found a tenant who absolutely loved the house and decided she wanted to move in. She didn't have all the down payment money. She only had half of it, but for me that was ok. Because she was going to give me the other half right? She told me she would. That was good enough for me. So we decided to go ahead and let her move in.

She was a single mother of two and a private investigator. I figured I could ask her to help me with some collections on some other tenants who weren't paying.

She moved in...and the bank started the foreclosure process back up. But they didn't send the notices to me...they sent it to the house.

So my tenant is now getting the foreclosure notices. She takes that to me that she doesn't have to pay rent anymore. So she didn't.

Three months later, after me saying "I know you're going through a hard time but you if you can just get the rent payment in at the end of this month that would great"...it never happened. I wanted to use the rent payments she should have been making to cover the other half of the down payment that my tenant never produced.

You see, the down payment she SAID she could make would have covered the arrearages to the bank and thus bring the loan current and do away with the foreclosure altogether. Because she only paid half when she moved in, I was counting on her monthly rent check each month in order to save enough to catch up the loan payments. I never got the chance.

Three months later we decided that it was time to evict her. We'd heard that an eviction would be a very time consuming and expensive process. Not this one. It was free. The county had already taken care of it for me. Because we didn't own the house anymore.

The bank had foreclosed and had kicked my tenant out on the street. My tenant said "You know what, I don't think you ever owned the house to begin with. So instead of the $5,000 deposit that I gave you I'm thinking, I'm thinking, I want $20,000 back. I've been through a lot. So if you'll just pay me $20,000 I'll leave you alone."

And I said "You know, that kind of sounds little like extortion. So I don't think I'm going to pay it. And I think you know where you can go and you know what you can do when you get there."

And she knew where she could go! She went to her locals process server and had him draw up paperwork to sue me.

For theft by deception.

And for those of ya'll that don't know theft by deception is not only a civil charge it's a criminal charge.

So, mother of three, living in a basement, government's paying for my food and the next thing I know, I'm sitting in front of two of Gwinnett County's finest mortgage fraud detectives trying to explain why I did what I did and the results of what occurred.

At any given time they could have said, "You know what? We really don't believe you. We don't think it went down the way it did, so why don't you just come on with us over to the 'pokey' and we'll get you processed and taken care of?"

I was scared to death. You guys don't want to know what it's like, sitting in front of those two detectives, getting sued. The worst I'd ever done was get a traffic ticket!

Why don't they teach life in college?

So what did I learn? Get everything in writing. In fact, the one thing, the one piece of paper that kept me out of jail...**it was Ron LeGrand's CYA Letter**.

Before the detectives got to my attorney's office, my attorney and I were sitting there going through all the paperwork that both the tenant and I AND the paperwork that the seller and I had signed.

Realize that we were borrowing money from the gentleman whose basement we were living in, in order to defend ourselves. My attorney is sitting there, going through the paperwork, and he says, "What's this?"

And I said "That's the deed transferring the title over to me."

"What's this?"

"That's the CYA letter saying that the homeowner, the seller is not going to sue me in case the house goes into foreclosure."

(He said, "We'll keep that out.")

"What's this?"

"That's the lease agreement."

"What's this?"

"That's the option agreement."

"What's this?"

"That's CYA letter saying that the tenant is not going to sue me if the house goes into foreclosure."

My attorney's eyes light up. He leans over to the phone on his desk, presses a button and says, "Laura, I'm going to need you to come in here and make 6 copies of this please."

And I could tell the tides had gotten ready to turn. The detectives arrived at the office and...you know that whole thing innocent until proven guilty thing?...It doesn't work that way. These were the meanest cops I have ever dealt with – but in their mind, they had a reason to be.

Keep in mind that I love all of our police and our firefighters. I love what they do for us on a daily basis, keeping us safe. The reason for the detectives to act the way they did was because they believed I had done something illegal and were not happy about it.

You see, these two gentlemen that I was sitting across from just **knew** that I was a dirty, stinking, rotten, investor that had taken advantage of somebody's situation. I had run off with a single mother's income and they were going to make sure that I paid for everything that I had done.

So we're sitting there and they pull out their paperwork and they said "Alright, what's this?"

And I said "That's the deed transferring title."

"What's this?"

"That's CYA letter saying the seller won't sue me if the house goes into foreclosure."

"What's this?"

"That's the lease agreement."

"What's this?"

"That's the option agreement."

"What's this?"

"That's the CYA letter saying the tenant won't sue me if the house goes into foreclosure."

And then the detectives did something I wasn't expecting...they stopped. They look at each other. Then one of them says, "Your tenant didn't give us this when she gave us all the paperwork that you two signed together."

My attorney leans back in his chair, crosses his arms and rather gleefully says, "Oh really!?!" I'm sitting there thinking, "Don't antagonize them. Okay? I don't' want to go to jail!"

The bottom line is you've got to get everything in writing. So how can you apply this to subprime investing?

The Intimidation Factor

Protect your chips. Life and investing, it's a big poker game. If you are not watching what's on the table, somebody's hands are going to be in your chips.

I recently had the absolute pleasure of read Robert Ringer's, "Winning Through Intimidation". It was one of the most phenomenal books I have ever read in my entire life. It's not in print anymore but at www.amazon.com you can pick it up.

In the book, Robert talks about 3 different types of people you're going to deal with in business.

Type #1 is the person that says I'm out for your chips and I just want you to know straight up front.
Type #2 is the kind that says I want you to have everything that you deserve but in reality I'm going to steal your chips.

Type #3 is the one that with all of the goodness in their heart says I want you to have everything that's coming to you. But in someway or circumstance they still wind up stealing your chips.

The whole point is that in real estate there are people out there that are going to try and make sure that you don't make the money that you deserve.

- ✓ Whether it's your family members talking about how real estate doesn't really work.
- ✓ Whether it's your friends saying "What the big deal with real estate anyway? Please! That's just a fly by night thing. If you <u>really</u> want to get in on something it needs to be selling cosmetics because it's the next big thing."
- ✓ Whether it's the seller that says "We didn't know you'd be making so much on this house! Maybe I should have asked for a little bit more."

- ✓ Or maybe it's your buyer that goes, "That's your bottom line? You don't deserve to make that much! I should get a little bit of this!"

You've got to protect your chips. That's one of the most important things you can do and that's what Robert Ringer talks about in his book.

So let me ask you this...I'm getting sued. I'm in a basement. I've no job. I have no money. Can it get any worse? It can always get worse. You're about to see just how much worse it can get!

Chapter 4

A Basement Full of Crap

WHEN MY FAMILY WAS LIVING IN THAT 200 SQUARE FOOT BASEMENT, WE SLEPT ON MATTRESSES PLACED ON THE FLOOR. I didn't have bed frames for the mattresses that we had.

We officially decided things had gotten 'worse' when woke up one morning to find that our mattresses were literally floating in two feet of raw sewage. The septic tank had backed up. Terrific!

I'll spare you most of the details. Needless to say, everything that had been less than 2 feet off the floor was ruined. The computer, all the mattresses, any clothes in the closet that had pants or long dresses that hung down, all of our shoes...you get the picture.

Our friend (the owner of the house) put us up in a local hotel for a couple of days until things could...settle down. We came back each day to bleach, clean, and sanitize. The last thing we could afford was for anyone to get sick from the disease that was possible in a situation like that one.

I was in the middle of a lawsuit, I didn't know the cops were going to come at any given time. I couldn't provide for my family. Why WOULDN'T I wake up in a basement full of crap?

The fact of the matter was those were really bad times. I mean, I don't think ya'll even realize those were awful, awful times.

When life gives you manure...
...you open a fertilizer store!

We went about trying to find a way to get out of our current situation and make money in the process.

We had to pull the carpet out. It ruined everything else I had in the basement. Any files that I had kept, all my deals, all the paperwork in them, they were sitting on the floor. So I couldn't read any of those. All paperwork I had was all destroyed.

I didn't have a backup plan. (Remember what I talked about earlier??? I violated lesson number one!) I didn't what I was going to do.

I got into my friends car and I just took a drive. At that point there was nothing I could do at the house that was going to make anything even remotely better about what I was dealing with. I had to go. I said "I'll be back." And I was gone.

As I was driving, I drove past my local library. I said, "How long has that been there? You know that's a quiet place I'm going to run in there."

While I was in there I got my library card. It was the only thing we could afford at the time. I once heard someone once say that if, if anybody had robbed me at the time, they would have been practicing. That's the truth of the matter. We didn't have anything.

So, I get my library card and discover that the library, unlike major book stores, you can take books without paying and read them and take them back and get more. That though had never occurred to me.

I had not been in a library since I was in like middle school. So I start checking out books by Zig Zigler and Bryan Tracy and Robert Kiyosaki and Donald Trump and Dan Kennedy and one fantastic and inspirational author after another. I also picked up real estate books by Robert Allen, Russ Whitney, Ron LeGrand, and others. I devoured them all!

I'm listening to these guys say to me, "You know what? You are in a really crappy situation right now but you are worth so much more. You deserve so much more than you've go right now. You only the way you are going to get there is massive simultaneous action."

"You've got to just get up, dust yourself off and say you know what that was really bad. Admittedly that was a bad thing to happen."

My dad always said, "If you're gonna be stupid, you gotta be tough!"

And eventually I realized, I'm not going to let any of this stop me! Not the lawsuit, not the basement full of crap, not anyone or anything!

My husband and I realized it was just as far to go back as it was to go forward. So we had a choice, standing in our basement full of crap. You can either move forward, or you can go back.

The fact was if I chose going back, it meant that I had to ask permission to go to the bathroom. I had to beg my supervisor to let me have the day after Thanksgiving off to spend with my family. I have to ask my son's school permission for him to go on a trip to see his grandparents because they don't want him missing too many days of school. I have to ask permission for everything.

And you know what? The truth is that I'm a 32 year old woman and I don't have to ask permission to do anything!

Moving forward meant that I can <u>do</u> whatever the heck I want to <u>when</u> I want to do it <u>how</u> I want to do it because **I'm** the one making the money! Because **I'm** the one responsible for putting food on my family's table! Because **I'm** the one that's going to be financially free! And because, DAMN IT, I'm sick and tired of living like an animal!

That's what happened and we decided to we decided to move forward with gusto, 100% in our real estate investing. We took advantage of our awful situation and started buying selling houses the way that we we're trained.

But this time, we were doing it properly, closing in an attorney's office and getting in writing everything, every single time. We were able to move out of the basement into our dream house.

Now ya'll recognize when I say 'dream house' I'm not talking about some 5,600 square foot house in a mansion in the suburbs somewhere.

My dream house is on 3 acres of prime farm land in the Middle of Nowhere, Georgia. I can't see anybody's house from mine.

Ya'll recognize that a Mercedes is not a Mercedes to everybody. My husband drives a Ford F250 Diesel truck. It's the loudest most unwomanly truck I have ever ridden in. But that's his dream car and I'm okay with that.

We took advantage of our situation and decided we weren't going to take it anymore. And we got out of that bad situation. So how do you apply it to real estate?

Take advantage and recognize an opportunity when you see one! In the next chapter, we'll take a look at one such opportunity...and I think you're gonna get excited when you read what it's about!

Chapter 5

The Subprime Opportunity's Knocking

WHEN AN OPPORTUNITY PRESENTS ITSELF YOU'RE GOING TO WANT TO TAKE ADVANTAGE OF IT. So let's look at some of the opportunities that are available to you now.

What about that one "S" word you keep hearing about on the news, on the radio, when you pick up the newspaper?

I'm talking about the subprime market. Everybody's familiar with subprime right? It's been on the news, in magazines and newspapers, on almost any channel you pick on TV! Just for the sake of argument, lets talk about what subprime is.

What is "Subprime"?

Borrowers with less than perfect credit history, also called 'B, C, and D credit'. These are NOT the folks that march down to Keller Williams or Remax or Century 21 and say "I'm looking to buy a house and I've already been down to Bank of America, they got me all taken care of all I've go to do is find a house."

Your typical subprime buyer can't go into your traditional Wachovia, Sun Trust and Bank of America and get a house. Subprime borrowers also have high risk characteristics like bankruptcy or collection accounts. I was about as high risk as they were going to get just a few short years ago!

Subprime borrowers could be considered 'risky' if they've had a bankruptcy within the past 5 years. There are some subprime lenders that can get a borrower approved within 12 months of a bankruptcy. The subprime lender can even get the borrower approved the day after the bankruptcy is discharged if they've been making on time payments while they're in bankruptcy.

Other Subprime characteristics are 'tough credit'. Some subprime loan symptoms are usually that they have high interest rates, a lot of times they'll have a pre-payment penalty. I think the most common example is the 2/28 adjustable rate mortgage (ARM). That's where you get fixed low, low teaser payments for the first 2 years and then after the 2nd year they can just sky rocket. There's a ceiling of course but the payments can start adjusting and adjusting and adjusting until you were once paying $600 bucks one month and the next thing you know you're paying $1800 and you don't know what happened.

A lot of times the folks will get a 2/28 loan because it's what with the understanding that they're going to hang onto it for the 2 years and make those incredibly low payments and the just refinance into another loan program.

The problem is refinancing a subprime loan into a prime loan are the prepayment penalties. You're going to pay an arm and a leg in that.

Subprime Statistics

I want to look at some statistics dealing with subprime. I'm trying to give you guys the most up to date information possible so that you can move forward with your real estate investing being on that cutting edge of what's going on.

The second largest subprime lender in the nation filed for Chapter 11 in April of 2007. Forty of their closest friends were doing it too. Why? Because all of a sudden these people with bad credit weren't paying.

Who saw that coming? :)

The borrowers weren't paying and they were falling into default. And all of a sudden New Century looks and says "You know what? We're going to wind up taking all these houses back!"

Here's just a little education on the whole banking industry for you...

Banks can only lend out based on the performing assets they have at any given time. And I know you've probably heard of this in any short sale seminar you've been to. So they don't want to take the houses back. Those are non performing assets. The house isn't generating interest on the money loaned out. If New Century started taking all the loans and houses back, I mean we're talking at least into the billions (with a "B") worth of dollars of property. They won't have anything to lend out. Nothing. So they filed for Chapter 11.

It's estimated that over 3 million homes across the United States will go into foreclosure in 2007 as a result of the subprime loans. **Three million.** How many investors want a piece of that action? Oh yea, that's a lot of houses!

Just think about the folks who are not going into foreclosure because they are struggling to keep their head above water and aren't willing to default yet! It's coming. Let those payments adjust a little bit more, and it will beyond what the borrowers have available. And over the next two years it's going to get worse and worse.

So Fannie Mae and Freddie Mac stepped in and said "You know, we realize that a lot of this stuff is going on and so we're going to implement some programs we set aside for just such an occasion." They collect something like ten billion dollars in order to help these folks who have been victim of the subprime industry get back on their feet. It's a stay of execution. Its just delaying the inevitable. It's still going to happen. Because let's face it they still have B & C & D credit. Their rates are still going to adjust. And they still aren't going to be able to make payments.

I've had so many tenants in this situation. So I'm speaking with a certain level of experience if you will. The people with Freddie Mac said "We're going to step in and help these folks out." What's going to happen in 6 months when the payments adjust again? Or the homeowner's car breaks down? Or the tax value on the house goes up?

Here's the problem. There are over 2 trillion dollars, (that's trillion with a "T") worth of adjustable rate mortgages that are going to start adjusting in 2007. That's a lot of zeros. More than Fannie Mae and Freddie Mac have set aside.

> How about he Fair Lending Act in Georgia and New Jersey? In 2002 New Jersey and Georgia instituted these Fair Lending Acts so that they could squash some the predatory lending that was going on. It is with a great sense of pride (read: sarcasm) that I tell you that Georgia is not only first but also third in the nation as far as counties go for mortgage fraud. We weren't content with just having one. We had to go first <u>and</u> third.

The Fair Lending Acts were an attempt to try and squash predatory lending. Within 6 months of these acts being created (in both states) they had to amended them because it was driving all of the subprime lenders out of the State of Georgia and the State of New Jersey. As a result they weren't exactly Fair Lending Acts at all.

There are a whole lot of problems and issues within the subprime industry going on right now. I mean if you guys turn on even 5 minutes of CNBC in the mornings you're seeing this stuff on a regular basis.

> In the 4th quarter of last year, that's October to December of 2006, 13% of all subprime borrowers made late payments. That's the highest delinquency rate in the past 4 years. In the 1st quarter of 2007? 43% of all subprime borrowers were in some form of delinquency. If you took 43% of 2 trillion dollars, that's a lot of money!

That's a lot of money out there not only for the banks who are struggling to not want to take these houses back, but also potential sellers for real estate investors like us who know to buy books like the one you're reading now in order to continue their education.

Chapter 6

Decisions, Decisions, Decisions!

SO, WHAT CAN YOU DO? The first thing is to do nothing.

It's not your problem right? It's not your job to try and save the world.

Last week we had like this horrendous storm in Georgia. It was bad. I was scared. We live in the middle of no where and there's nothing but really huge trees on my property.

We woke up Sunday morning and we had no power. We wound up at a Hardee's (like Jack-in-the-

Box or Carl's Jr). My husband's paying with a credit card. So while I'm grabbing breakfast, my husband hands his credit card to the cashier behind the counter. He goes to hand her his driver license to verify his ID with the credit card and she says "Oh don't worry about that. I mean, if it your credit card gets stolen it'ain't my concern!" Wow. I felt so much better about eating there!

But the fact of the matter is, it **is** your job. It **is** your problem. There are over 3 million victims of subprime lending in the United States today that are depending on folks like us to get them out of the situation that they're in.

Do you remember earlier I was talking about the folks who were going to tell you that you can't make money in real estate? The folks that are going to say, "Well you know that's cute and all but, I don't know that you're going to be able to retire based on what you do"... The fact is my family is just like that.

My mom calls me every single month and asks me if she needs to send me money. My dad doesn't ask that because he was my private lender one time and he knows better.

But the fact of the matter is, it is your job and it is your problem. And the fact is that you're able to do something about it. I said, "What can I do? You know, I can sit back and look at a deal and say, 'Well, there's really not enough profit in this for me to risk getting involve so I'm going to pass on it."

And all of a sudden I realize with all these subprime loans coming in I'm throwing away more than I'm going after!

I don't know if ya'll have picked up on this or not, but I like having money around. I've been rich and I've been poor and I can tell you that being rich is a lot better. You can do more and you can go more places and you can see more when you've got money and I am never going to be in the situation that we were in where I could not afford to give my family what they wanted and needed.

So I said, "How can I take advantage of the situation? How can open my own fertilizer store, if you will?" Because we all that 'one guy' that's going to take advantage of people in a bad situation. What's he going to do? He's going to be a jerk and he's going to wring every single penny that that buyer and seller has out of the deal and he's going to hang them out to dry and he's going to walk away with the money when all he could have done is just one little change to be able to help the people in that bad situation.

I'm a big proponent of ethics in investing. Now for those of you who don't know, ethics is a dirty little word that's creeping back into the real estate industry.

Last year, I was reading an article about some folks in California who were trying to sell their house and it was this cute little old lady and this little old man and the reporter said, "Well, why do you think you are having trouble selling?" (It was right when the California market started to take a nose dive.)

And this little old lady says, "I don't know why we haven't been able to sell our house, but I feel like the market is punishing us as if we were real estate investors." **Punishing us.** She was talking about us. She was talking about you and I.

Who's afraid of the BBB?

We have the reputation of a used car salesman right now. Remember "Honest Larry's Real Estate Investment Business"? So what can we do?

Are you a member of your local Chamber of Commerce? Let me ask you this, do you have any idea of what goes on at a Chamber of Commerce meeting? There are a couple of things that I like about my Chamber...

First, they give you a microphone. I'm a big fan of anybody that will give me a microphone. I'm a member of the largest Chamber of Commerce, the most active in the state of Georgia. So every single week, a hundred of my closest friends get together in a room and they give me a microphone for 30 seconds and they say, "Go for it!"

I get to stand up and I have to pick what I'm going to say.

? Do I want to talk about how I've helped folks who have gotten into a bad situation, be able to get out quickly, out from under their debt and sell their house?

? Do I talk about how I can help buyers because of my unique financing options, lease option, rent to own plans? And if you think the Realtors in the room are not burning up the paper, writing down my information, you're nuts!

? Or do I talk about the fact that anybody unhappy with their current rate of return on their CD's, their money market accounts or 401k's, can earn 15% or higher by investing in me with real estate. Which do I talk about?

I just rotate through them every single week. I talk about something else each time. And you know what? I'm the only investor there which means not only am I the resident expert, but I also get all the leads. I get more leads from my Chamber of Commerce than I do from the bandit signs that I put out.

Okay, so we talked about being a member of your Chamber of Commerce. Are you a member of your Better Business Bureau? Why?

When you send out your direct mail and your seller gets it and opens it up and looks at it, once to the bottom of the page, it says, "Member of the Better Business Bureau and Chamber of Commerce." Number one, it builds credibility. (Remember Honest

Joe's Real Estate Investing Company?) Number two, you are giving the buyers and sellers permission to check up on you.

I'm going to say that again. You are giving them permission to check up on you.

When you leave from meeting with the seller, (especially when you are buying sub2) and you're trying to talk about the loan staying in their name and you make the payments...contrary to popular belief, a lot of folks aren't just like, you know, 'kicking up their heels with excitement' about that one.

When you leave the seller's house, they can pick up the phone or go on line and check up on you and see if you really do what you say you're gong to do! Having that one step in place will dramatically increase the conversions that you get from leads to actual prospect, increasing the number of houses that you actually buy.

The Chamber of Commerce and the Better Business Bureau...those are two vitally important memberships that you need become a part of immediately.

I want to back up and talk about direct mail because I know that when I said direct mail, half of my readers were like, "Oh my God! It doesn't work because it was too hard. It won't work in my area. It's too expensive."

Let me ask you this...If you send out your direct mail in white number ten envelopes that look just like all of the other mail that the seller has been getting...and you borrowed a letter from a boot camp manual that 300 of your closest friends got and 300 of the friends that attended the boot camp before you and 300 of the friends that attended the boot camp after you got...and the seller goes and checks the mail and the first letter from an investor says, "We want to buy your house." The second letter says, "We want to buy your house." And the letter says, "We want to buy your house." All the letters are the same. It's just the name is changed at the end.

Do you think you are going to get the lead from anybody? No!

You've got to stand out and be different. You got to make yourself so completely different from your competition, that the seller has absolutely no reason not to call you.

Chapter 7

Getting the phone to ring

ONE OF THE WAYS YOU CAN GET YOUR PHONE TO RING OFF THE HOOK WITH MOTIVATED SELLERS WANTING TO SELL YOU THEIR HOUSE... (I'M GOING TO SCARE YOU)... IS TO WRITE YOUR OWN DIRECT MAIL LETTERS. Don't you have to be Shakespeare or Hemingway to write your own direct mail letters? It's not true!

You've got to be able to put yourself in the seller's shoes. And this is the one thing that everyone else who buys this book hopes you don't read and go home and implement right away. You don't send one letter to one seller and then go on to another list. When I said *massive simultaneous action*, I mean you hit them three, four and seven times.

You never, ever mail to one person on one list, one time. Three, four, seven times . . . seven is the most that I've ever done. My longest letter has been 16 pages. Now we've moved into you saying . . . "I would never read 16 pages. Oh my God!"

First of all, you've probably never been a motivated seller, okay? And if you have, I am not saying to start writing to people and with a postcard that says,

"We want to buy your house. Are you upsizing? Downsizing? Behind on payments? Divorced? Pre foreclosure? Bankruptcy? Death in the family? 1-800-ME-TOO-ME-TOO. We can help."

That postcard is a no-no! You should be sending out one letter, to one situation. If they are in pre-foreclosure, then my letter talks about how much it sucks going out to the mailbox every single day to have to carry back all of the letters from the lenders, the investors, and the realtors who all just happen to be in the neighborhood and want to stop by and talk to you.

It is about being afraid to answer the phone because you know it's going to be the lender who has turned into some kind of mafia boss demanding HIS money.

It's not wanting to go to the door because if one more person knocks on the door and says, "Hey, I just happened to be in the neighborhood. Have you got a second?" You're going to shoot yourself. People are getting bombarded on a regular basis, especially the ones in pre-foreclosure. You've got to hammer that home in your mailings.

I do not advocate writing to active listings, but if they're an expired listing in the multiple listing system. That's the best ones that I can think of. They have been trying to sell their house for six or twelve months, have their hand up, "Please!

Somebody buy my house! And they haven't been able to sell it yet.

Why not you? Why don't you buy it? They've got pretty houses and junker houses in the MLS. I know. I looked. Talk about how frustrating that is that they couldn't move on with their life, put their kid in a new school district. They have to make six months worth of utility payments and maintenance payments and chauffeur people in and outside their house at all hours of the day.

Talk about the fact that their house seems perfectly fine to them, but all of a sudden the buyers want a carpet allowance and a paint allowance and they want you to re-landscape the back yard. They want a survey. They want an inspection. Talk about all of that stuff!

One letter, one situation

Mail up to seven times. That sounds like a lot of work, doesn't it? Doesn't it? You can tell me.

Isn't that a lot of work? "You mean I've got to write seven letters for one situation and then start mailing? I don't even like getting my hands dirty on a rehab, let alone sitting down to write seven letters."

The fact of the matter is, when I was sitting in my basement and I was depending on the government to pay for my food, and I had to decide whether or not I was going to eat or market my business. It still sounded like a lot of work.

Massive simultaneous action. This stuff is not get rich quick. Heck, sometimes it's not even get rich if you don't do it right. Sometimes you just got to suck it up and do it.

Yes, it's going to sound like a lot of work. Yes, it's going to require some of your time.

Here's the fact of the matter. When you decided to become a real estate investor, especially if you quit your job because you're going to become a real estate investor, you're now your own boss... it's now up to you to decide whether or not you're actually going to get up every morning, implement something new that's going to bring in leads or to decide, "You know what? I am my own boss. I don't really feel like getting up this morning and if I do feel like getting up this morning and go hit a couple of rounds of golf, I am my own boss. I can do whatever I want."

It's having a daily schedule. It's having a structure. It's not only having a business plan. It's having a marketing plan, where you know where exactly where your leads are going to come from each and every month.

This is a business and here's the problem. When you got started in real estate investing, the folks that go out and start a Kinko's franchise or a Subway or whatever, they get trained. Right?

People tell them that these are the things that you need to do everyday. This is the education that you are going to need. Go forth and get it done.

When you become a real estate investor, nobody tells you this stuff. Right? You get out there and you start winging it and you go, "Oh my gosh! Nobody told me it was going to be this hard! Nobody told me that I had to do all this work!"

I mean this with the most love and sincerity as possible. You can fall off the turnip truck and be a real estate investor. Right? That's what I did! I woke up one morning and said it was going to be a real estate investor. How hard can it be, just buy and sell houses!

It's not that easy. It's hard work! That's why we home school our kids so they can see there's no magic button on the printer where the money starts shooting out.

They get up in the middle of the night and sometimes I'm still sitting in front of the laptop. I've met with sellers in the middle of the night before.

I had one seller whose son was getting married and they drove down from New Jersey to Atlanta and was still trying to sell their house and the only time they had to meet with me was at midnight. So I took myself and my husband-appointed-bodyguard and we went down and we met with them, in the middle of the night! I came back at 2:00 AM with a contract.

So I said, number one, you can do nothing. You can do nothing all you want because that just means that I'm going to buy and sell more houses this year.

Chapter 8

Graduate Magna Cum Laude of the School of Hard Knocks!

YOUR SECOND OPTION IS TO GRADUATE MAGNA CUM LAUDE OF THE SCHOOL OF HARD KNOCKS. That's what I did. I went out and made all the mistakes on my own. It was easy to do. There were plenty of them to be made.

I didn't even tell you half the stuff that I went through, getting to the point where I'm at. It was tough. And you can do it. It can be done.

I'm living proof that you can do it...but it's gonna cost ya! I've spent $25,000 defending myself in that lawsuit. Now we won because stupid is not illegal fortunately...Yet. Even in the state of Georgia.

The fact of the matter is, I couldn't just say, "You know. I'll just give my tenant the money and she'll go away and I won't have to go through this entire headache." Because the next time a real estate investor winds up in court, the judge is going to go back and say, "Well, I see in Young vs. So-and-So that they settled out of court which is kind of the same thing as admitting guilt. So I'm going to use that to weigh my decision." And the investor after that and the investor after that.

And I knew that if I didn't stand up for myself, that it could potentially effect more folks down the line.

So you can go to the School of Hard Knocks and still get it done. But you've got one more option at your disposal...(a much easier and quicker option!)

Chapter 9

Subprime Secrets

SO YOU CAN DO NOTHING...OR YOU CAN CREATE YOUR OWN PATH, BLAZE YOUR OWN TRAIL, AND MAKE TONS OF POTENTIALLY FATAL MISTAKES ALONG THE WAY...OR YOU CAN FOLLOW THE EDUCATION PROVIDED BY SOMEONE WHO'S ALREADY BEEN THERE. In this particular situation, that happens to be me because I am the one they gave the task of writing this book to.

I'm talking about Subprime Secrets. This is a system that I came up with because, remember I told you I got sick and tired of throwing away all the leads that came across my desk because they were all 100% financed, or they were over financed, or they were over financed and paid way too much every month?

I said, "What can I do?" So I sat down and figured it out. I got to motivate sellers to call me. When you deal with anything that I offer or whether it's my coaching program or any of my other materials...if you're doing cold calls or knocking on doors, it is not because I taught you. If it's working, please, by all means, don't stop, okay? ONLY If it's working for you.

But I say there are better things that you can do with your time. Because your time is worth a whole lot more than you are giving it credit for than to go out and knock on doors and make cold calls, especially when making cold calls.

The fact of the matter is that when you go through handling some of the calls yourself, the first phone call you make starts off like, "Hey, I was just calling because I heard that you guys might be in a bad situation and I wanted to offer you an alternative so that we can help get you out of that."

By the third and fourth phone call, you've heard so many "no's", you're like, "I'm sure that you're not going to go for this, but . . ." right? You're dejected! Because it stinks!

So I get the folks to call me. They raise their hand first. And then I look at it and decide whether or not it's a deal for me. I call everybody back, but I decide whether or not I'm going to call them back and say, "Hey, let's more forward." Or "This is not necessarily a deal for me, however, I got one of the most phenomenal real estate agents on the planet who can help you sell your house."

Always call everybody back. Why do you think I say that? Your reputation is number one. Here's the thing, what happens when one of your leads calls in and you look at it and you're like, "Wow, I'm not touching this one with a ten foot pole." And you don't call them back. They call you a couple of times because they always do, right? They say, "Hey, I'm just calling because nobody called me back the first time." Then, "Hey, I'm just calling because nobody called me back the second time." They keep calling and eventually they go away.

So imagine your seller (the one you didn't call back because it wasn't a good deal) is standing next to a white picket fence separating her house from the neighbors. The neighbor comes over and says, "I know that you know about the situation we're in, but I got this letter from these folks and it really looks like they can help. I'm thinking about calling them to sell our house."

And the seller you refused to call back says, "Personally, I tried to call them several times last month and they never returned my phone calls. I wouldn't waste your time."

You lost the lead before you even knew you had it! All it takes is a phone call. Okay? So always follow up with everybody.

I can pre-screen each seller in five minutes or less, based on the checklist and the worksheets and the system that I put into place. I call it a guaranteed system and you're going to see why in a minute. I can choose the best way to buy because I've got several buying strategies in my arsenal. The scoring system that we use, it's kind of like playing video games where you're always trying to up your best score. (My kids are totally addicted to video games would appreciate that reference immensely.)

So what are you going to get?

With my system, Subprime Secrets, the first thing that you're going to get are 8 (eight) interactive DVD's. There's no boot camp because this is the boot camp. And it's not me speaking in a room full of people. This is me talking directly to you.

They're interactive DVD's where I go through each step of the system. I do a seller presentation and I also do live seller calls while the camera is rolling. You get to hear exactly what the seller said, exactly what I said and how I was able to screen them and decide whether or not to make an appointment. Put them in your DVD player or in your computer and watch. Now, I kept in mind that not everybody wants to sit there for eight hours and watch me. Even my husband said, "After DVD #2, I've got to take a break for a little while because I see you everyday." So I put them on 8 CD's as well.

Eight CD's where you can sit there and listen in your car. Zig Zigler says turn your car into 'Automobile University'. And I've taken that step for you. They can also easily be convert to MP3's so your iPod becomes an educational experience. So you get to hear that as well.

I've also got two manuals and these are not thin manuals, where we go through each and every step.

All of the worksheets I talk about, the checklists, they are all included. You can watch them with the DVD's and they work in tandem or you can use them on their own.

I go through and interview one of the most successful real estate rehabbers on the planet. His name is Joe Brillante. And he can take trash and cash it in a heartbeat. So I sat down and find out how he does his stuff.

I also sat down with the best sub-to guy on the planet, Mike Brunett. If you don't get anything out of all of the materials I provide, that one interview will impact you so dramatically. It will change your life!

Mike is the most integrity-filled investor I've ever met. If you were faced with a seller who was struggling, who was in early stages of Alzheimer's, that didn't quite understand the numbers when it was put on paper...Would you would have taken him out to breakfast to sit down with the man and go over each and every line of the contract and spend the next four hours talking to him and explaining to him so he knew that he wasn't being taken advantage of? That's what Mike does. He takes better care of his buyers and sellers than anybody I've ever seen. I had to get an interview with him.

Finally, I talked with an investor that doesn't even buy houses. He saves them. He keeps people in their house and made $250,000 just on one deal. That's one DVD you DON'T want to miss!

So, that's ten hours of training. I also give you a 90-day subprime real estate marketing system. We go week by week and I give you a to-do list. Remember when I said *massive simultaneous action*?

Your to-do list will give you five different strategies to attract sellers, financed by subprime mortgages, five different strategies on any budget and using any buying strategy. I give you five different marketing techniques. I'll show you how to get the phone to ring with leads! There's very little involvement from you on this one. I found that when I answer the phone... (ladies, please don't be mad at me), but I've got diarrhea of the mouth. There's a little shock value for you.

I answer the phone and the next thing I know everything is coming out as fast as I can get it out. And I'm blowing the seller away and they're like, "Oh, my God. I don't know what you're talking about. We're going to have to think about it." So I've given you the same system I used to get folks to call me and what my voicemail actually says.

I also threw in a seven page report with my attorney who specializes in sub-to closings and land trusts and he demystifies some of that stuff for you as well.

So how much would you pay?

What if I told you over the next three years, you will pay $1.09 a day, would you be willing? Would you be interested?

That $1.09 a day breaks down into **three monthly payments of $393**. The total price of the package is $1,179, but I want you to be able to use the profits from the system in order to pay for the system itself. Okay?

So that would be $1.09 a day over the next three years...by making 3 investments of $393.

I do have a guarantee. I want you to take Subprime Secrets home and use it. If for any reason, whether I didn't come through with what I said, I don't care if you got a paper cut, send it back at any time over the next 90 days and I will refund 100% of what you pay. No questions asked. No flaming hoops to jump through. No forms to fill out.

When you purchase Subprime Secrets, I've included complimentary enrollment and one month free in my Inner Circle Gold program. Do you remember me saying, "Don't stop! Don't quit! Don't give up! Your very best, your very best!" That's what the Inner Circle Gold Program is.

Every single month, you will have me on the phone and I'm just as energetic in real life as I am on stage. You're going to see every single month, the new and latest marketing techniques to buy and sell property because we go over the different marketing methods each month. The last few months, we've done signs, we've done newspaper ads, we've done business cards, and we've done billboards.

We'll take one specific marketing strategy, rip it apart and create a better way to generate leads for your business. There's also a lot of motivational stuff as well because I'm a big fan of motivation.

I can be there on the phone with you every single month to cheer you on down the field. Before you know it, you're going to be in the end zone.

Here's what happens with the Inner Circle Gold program, I send you a newsletter at some point during the month. The newsletter has questions in it. You guys call in on the conference call and I'm on the conference call with you, we do it live and I will take your questions on the call every single month, whether it's marketing questions, whether it's real estate questions or it's life questions, I don't care. We'll tackle it all.

With your Inner Circle Gold Program, you also get a free copy of The Best of Big Cheese. My company is Big Cheese Marketing and I put together a manual for you with tips and tidbits.

You also get four audio CD's as well. In one, I'm being interviewed by another investor. There are pod cast and audio clips as well. I also interview my sign printer and my real estate agent on these Inner Circle CDs.

They do some stuff that you all didn't know about and I tell you what...***My real estate agent gives you one word that you can use with other agents to get a list of people interested in buying property where you have your house.*** One word.

You think I'm going to tell you what it is? It's on the CD.

Okay, so what motivates you more?

→ Those three million people that are going to be stuck in foreclosure this year? The victims of sub-prime lending?
→ That jerk we talked about who is going to take advantage of the people in this situation? How's that for motivation?
→ The government . . . we didn't even talk about that yet!

Congress is in meetings to talk about reform for subprime loans. What happens when the government gets involved in our businesses? The little guy suffers and the true criminals are never brought to justice. They're meeting right now to discuss our fate.

You can make money hand over fist while potentially changing someone's life. Subprime Secrets will teach you the basics on how to buy and sell houses. But more importantly, this is all about marketing. What happens when marketing is not there?

You can have the best buy and selling education on the planet, but if the leads aren't coming in, you ain't buying a house, okay?

So this is mainly talking marketing. I give you a checklist for you to use, based on the score that you get, and know how to buy and sell that property. I also give you recommended vendors in case there is a strategy that we cover that you're not familiar with.

Everything you need is in here, regardless of how you're motivated, whether it's your pocketbook or status, being able to show your mother-in-law that their kid didn't marry a deadbeat after all, regardless of whether it's buying that nice house or nice car.

Subprime Secrets is what you need to succeed so my question to you is what are you guys waiting for? It's all here. Go to www.subprimesecrets.com and order your copy today!

Keep the momentum going!

Now that you've learned more about the opportunities available to you in today's real estate market, it's time to up the ante and join the Big Cheese Inner Circle Gold program!

All you have to do is go to www.bigcheesemarketing.com/inner-circle.htm and sign up today!

(Or you can use the form at the end of this book to get one month FREE!)

Recommended Resources

Please visit our website,

www.bigcheesemarketing.com

to review:

- ✓ Additional information about our real estate marketing products.
- ✓ Frequently Asked Questions (FAQ's) about our products.
- ✓ Big Cheese Marketing and Rachel Young's appearances and interviews

Thank You

About the Author

From humble beginnings in as the oldest of 4 children living in a 1 bedroom trailer, to homeless single mother of 3, Rachel Young has certainly seen her share of hard times. Her drive, determination, and spectacular marketing abilities brought her "up from the ashes" and led her to being one of Atlanta's most successful real estate investors in single family homes.

Rachel's willingness to teach her strategies and marketing techniques to others has made her a much sought-after business woman in the real estate investing community. She is an investor as well as an entrepreneur. Her company, Big Cheese Marketing has customers in all 50 states as well as countries around the world.

A Special Free Gift from the Author!

Copy this page and Fax this Form to:

678-348-7228

FREE

Test Drive 30 Full Days of Rachel Young's

Big Cheese Inner Circle Gold Program

Receive a steady stream of marketing and real estate building advice.

Yes Rachel, I want to take you up on your offer of a FREE 30 Day Inner Circle Gold Program Membership, which includes:

1. One full month of The Cheese Grater Newsletter
2. One full month of audio teleseminar
3. Special FREE Call-in Times
4. Open fax line
5. At least 25% discount to future Big Cheese events and seminars

There is a one time charge of $19.97 that will be waived when you fax in your order form. Even after your FREE 30 days, you have no obligation to continue at the lowest Gold Member price of $47.97 per month. In fact, should you continue with membership, you can cancel at any time by calling Big Cheese Marketing Inner Circle at 678-448-4068 or faxing a cancellation note to 678-348-7228.

Don't worry about ruining your book. A photocopy works just fine. ☺

Name____

Address ____

☐ Business ☐ Home

City/State/Zip ____________________ Email ________________

Phone __________________________ Fax __________________

Credit Card

☐ Visa ☐ MasterCard ☐ American Express

Credit Card # __________________________ Exp date _____

Signature ____________________________ Date _________

Providing this information constitutes your permission for Big Cheese Marketing, LLC to contact you regarding information via mail, e-mail, fax, and phone.